12 CREEPY
URBAN LEGENDS

by Kenya McCullum

12
STORY
LIBRARY

www.12StoryLibrary.com

12-Story Library is an imprint of Peterson Publishing Company and Press Room Editions.

Produced for 12-Story Library by Red Line Editorial

Photographs ©: tobkatrina/Shutterstock Images, cover, 1; Jemny/Shutterstock Images, 4; AP Images, 5; DragoNika/Shutterstock Images, 6; Photographee.eu/Shutterstock Images, 7, 17; Kristin Smith/ Shutterstock Images, 9, 28; Darryl Brooks/Shutterstock Images, 10; Niloo/Shutterstock Images, 11; Everett Collection/Shutterstock Images, 12, 29; Monkey Business Images/Shutterstock Images, 13; Steve Debenport/iStockphoto, 14; eldinhoid/iStockphoto, 15; bravobravo/iStockphoto, 16; luiggi33/ Shutterstock Images, 18; Wehands/iStockphoto, 19; Vasilyev Alexandr/Shutterstock Images, 20; Dennis W. Donohue/Shutterstock Images, 21; Ariwasabi/Shutterstock Images, 22; DW Labs Incorporated/ Shutterstock Images, 23; Johann Viloria/Shutterstock Images, 24; scull2/iStockphoto, 25; Air Images/ Shutterstock Images, 26; subhasish/iStockphoto, 27

Library of Congress Cataloging-in-Publication Data
Names: McCullum, Kenya, 1972- author.
Title: 12 creepy urban legends / by Kenya McCullum.
Other titles: Twelve creepy urban legends
Description: Mankato, MN : 12-Story Library, 2017. | Series: Scary and spooky
  | Includes bibliographical references and index.
Identifiers: LCCN 2016002348 (print) | LCCN 2016006720 (ebook) | ISBN
  9781632352927 (library bound : alk. paper) | ISBN 9781632353429 (pbk. :
  alk. paper) | ISBN 9781621434580 (hosted ebook)
Subjects: LCSH: Urban folklore--Juvenile literature. | Legends--Juvenile
  literature.
Classification: LCC GR78 .M35 2016 (print) | LCC GR78 (ebook) | DDC
  398.2--dc23
LC record available at http://lccn.loc.gov/2016002348

Printed in the United States of America
Mankato, MN
May, 2016

Access free, up-to-date content on this topic plus a full digital version of this book. Scan the QR code on page 31 or use your school's login at 12StoryLibrary.com.

Table of Contents

A Man with a Hook Hand on the Loose

A teenage boy and girl sit in a car in a quiet area. They are having fun and listening to the radio. A news announcer suddenly comes on the air. The announcer says there is a dangerous criminal on the loose in the community. The announcer says the man has a hook for a hand.

The girl gets very scared and wants to go home. The boy thinks there is nothing to be afraid of. He does not want to leave. But the girl continues asking the boy to take her home.

The boy drives the girl home as fast as he can. When they get to the girl's house, the boy opens the car door for her. They are shocked to find a hook hanging on the car door handle. There are also scratches on the car door.

The story of the man with the hook for a hand may have first been seen in print on November 8, 1960. It

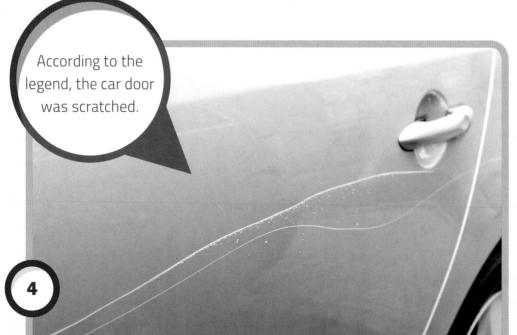

According to the legend, the car door was scratched.

appeared in the newspaper column Dear Abby. Someone wrote a letter to columnist Abigail Van Buren to tell the hook story. The reader believed the story was true and became fearful that teenagers who went out at night were not safe.

The story was nothing new, however. It had been told by teens around the country for years. Usually when the story was told, people said it happened in their own towns.

The urban legend became popular thanks to Van Buren's column.

1950s
Era when the hook story began.

- A girl and a boy hear on the radio that a criminal is on the loose.
- The man has a hook for a hand.
- When the boy takes the girl home, they find a hook on the car door handle.
- The story may have first been seen in print in the Dear Abby newspaper column.

CARS AND URBAN LEGENDS

Many urban legends have a car in the story. This is because so many people drive and own cars. It makes the story sound true. Urban legends may be about a car accident, buying an expensive car, or changing a flat tire. Other stories may be about a crime involving a car.

Choking Dog Saves Family

A woman receives a Doberman pinscher as a present from her husband. He chose this dog to protect the family. One day, the woman comes home to find the dog choking.

She rushes the dog to the veterinarian. The dog needs surgery, so the woman goes home. The phone is ringing when she opens the door. The vet is on the phone. He tells the woman to get out of the house right away. It is an emergency and he has already called the police.

The police arrive at the house and go inside. They find a burglar hiding in the closet with a few of his fingers missing. The police tell the woman the vet found the fingers in her dog's throat. This version of the story was first told in the 1980s. It became popular because some people are afraid of crime.

In another version of this story, the woman stays at the vet's office. When the vet finishes surgery, he shows the woman the fingers from the dog's throat. In some versions, the dog vomits up the fingers in front of the woman. Some people may use a different breed of dog when telling the story. But it is always a protective dog.

Dobermans are known to be protective guard dogs.

The dog attacks the burglar in this legend.

2
Number of fingers the legend claims were found in the dog's throat.

- A woman receives a Doberman pinscher for protection.
- One day, she finds her pet choking and takes it to the vet.
- The woman later finds out there were fingers in the dog's throat.
- The fingers belonged to a burglar who was caught in her home.

The original version of this urban legend is very different from the one that people tell today. The story began in Wales, United Kingdom. In the original version, a prince leaves a dog to guard his baby. When he returns home, the baby's crib is turned over. The dog is covered in blood. The prince punishes the dog, thinking it killed the baby. But later, the prince finds the baby safe, lying next to a dead wolf on the floor. The dog saved the baby from the wolf.

A Beehive Hairdo Attracts Many Bugs

In the 1950s, many girls wore their hair in a beehive hairdo. It was a popular style. Girls shaped their hair on top of their heads in a cone shape. It looked similar to a beehive.

One girl liked this hairstyle a lot. She put her hair into the perfect beehive. She was proud of it. She did not want to take it down. So the girl did not comb or wash her hair for many months. Soon, bugs began living in the girl's hair. One day, she died. The bugs had eaten through her skin to her brain.

In another story, a girl with a beehive hairdo is sitting in class. Blood starts running down her neck. Then the girl passes out. She is taken to the hospital. The doctor finds cockroaches in her hair. The cockroaches ate her brain, causing her to die.

Some stories have been told where the girl has spiders living in her beehive hairdo. Other times, people tell the story with bees.

One of the earliest versions of this story was told in England in the 1200s. In this urban legend, a woman in Oxfordshire, England, took

BUGS IN A CAST

Similar urban legends involving bugs do not have anything to do with hair. One story involves bugs in a cast. In this story, someone has a cast on an injured part of his or her body. The person keeps itching that area. The cast is taken off, and ants or termites are found inside it. The bugs had eaten the person's limb.

a long time getting ready for church. She was fixing her hair. One day, the devil turned into a spider and attacked her head. The spider would not leave her alone until a minister performed a religious ceremony to help her.

- A girl fixes her hair into a perfect beehive hairdo.
- She uses hairspray to keep it in place and stops washing her hair.
- Bugs get into her hair and eat through to her brain.
- Other versions of the story have cockroaches, spiders, or bees.

The beehive hairstyle was popular in the 1950s.

Man Accidentally Eats Fried Rat

People have been telling a story of a fried rat for decades. A man goes to a fast-food restaurant to order a bucket of fried chicken. As he is eating, he thinks the chicken tastes funny. He takes the breading off the chicken and realizes there is a rat inside.

In another version of this story, a woman is eating chicken in a car with her husband. The woman thinks there is something wrong with the chicken. Her husband cuts into it and finds a rat. The woman gets very sick. Her husband takes her to the hospital. After being in critical condition for a while, she dies.

Sometimes when people tell the story, a man and woman are eating the chicken by a fireplace. It is dark in the room. They take a few bites of the chicken. They do not like how it tastes. They turn on the light and see that it is a rat.

This story does not always involve chicken. In one urban legend, a

As fast food became more popular, so did urban legends similar to this story.

- A man goes to a fast-food restaurant and orders fried chicken.
- He finds a rat inside the breading after realizing it tastes funny.
- Another version of the story puts a woman in the hospital after she eats fried rat.
- Other stories have rats in soda and chocolate.

Soda is another food item popular in urban legends.

woman visits a chocolate factory. She watches candy being made. She notices a rat floating in a vat of chocolate.

There have also been tales about mice and soda. In these stories, people drink a soda and find pieces of mice in it. Sometimes there is a whole mouse in the bottle.

The fried rat story has been spreading since the 1970s. This was because more people were getting their meals from fast-food restaurants. The urban legend became more popular when talk show host Johnny Carson told a joke about it on *The Tonight Show*. The show aired on May 23, 1979.

LIFE IMITATES LEGEND

On February 3, 1971, *The Washington Post* reported that a man found a tail and the legs of a mouse in a bottle of Coca-Cola. He sued the company and the supermarket where he bought it. He claimed he got sick and had to go to the hospital after drinking the soda. He wanted $100,000 for his injuries. He received a $20,000 settlement from the companies.

5
The Devil Goes to a Dance

A handsome man enters a dance hall. He dances with many of the women in the hall that night. Later, one of the women dances with the man and looks down toward the floor. She notices the stranger has chicken feet. According to legend, this means that he is the devil. The woman screams and everyone at the dance hall becomes frightened. The man leaves in a cloud of smoke. He gets on a horse outside and rides away.

Another story tells of a young woman who goes dancing on a Sunday night. She meets a handsome stranger at the dance. They begin to dance together. One of the men playing music at the dance looks around. He sees that the stranger has hooves instead of feet. He tells the other musicians that the strange man is the devil. They start playing a religious song. The man continues dancing with the young girl. He twirls her around. She cannot stop moving. She spins, hits a window, and falls through. Then the handsome man disappears. This urban legend comes from European folklore.

According to the legend, everyone thought the man was a wonderful dancer.

Another version of the legend has the devil playing cards before disappearing.

Another urban legend about the devil takes place at a card game. Some men are playing cards in an old cabin. A stranger knocks on the door and asks if he can stay at the cabin. The owner of the cabin agrees. The stranger joins the men in the card game. He starts winning all their money. One man sees that the stranger has cloven hooves instead of feet. He becomes afraid and knocks over a kerosene lamp. The cabin catches on fire. The men run out of the house but the stranger stays inside. The men are afraid. They stay outside for the rest of the night. In the morning, they go back into the cabin. The strange man is gone.

12:00
Time of night when the devil begins spinning the young girl on the dance floor.

- A handsome man dances with all the beautiful women at a dance hall.
- One woman notices he has chicken feet, which means he is the devil.
- Another story tells of the devil spinning a woman so she cannot stop.
- The devil also appears in other stories involving a cabin and card games.

Clown Statue Frightens Babysitter

A couple goes to a party one night. They hire a babysitter to watch their children. After the children go to sleep, the babysitter watches television in the parents' bedroom.

People started telling the story of the clown statue and the babysitter in 2004.

She notices a clown statue in the room and becomes frightened. The babysitter calls the parents to ask if she can move the statue or put a sheet over it. The parents tell the babysitter to take the children to their neighbors' house and call the police. Then they say they do not own a clown statue. The police later find a man in a clown suit running in the neighborhood.

The clown statue story is not the only urban legend about a babysitter. In the 1970s, people began telling the story of a babysitter and the man upstairs. A babysitter puts the children to bed. The phone rings. A man on the phone asks her, "Have you checked on the children?" The man calls over and over again. The babysitter calls the police. They warn her to get out of the house. The police tell her that the calls were made from the phone upstairs.

There are more versions of this story. In one, the babysitter finds the intruder in the house. She runs outside and calls the police. In another tale, the babysitter runs out of the house and then calls the police. The police find out that one of the children was making the calls all along.

2
Number of children whom the babysitter puts to bed.

- When the children go to sleep, the babysitter notices a clown statue in the parents' bedroom.
- She calls the parents and they say they do not have a clown statue.
- Other babysitting stories involve people calling the house many times.
- Often these stories have an intruder in the house.

A Woman Is Buried Alive

After a woman dies, her husband has dreams about her. In the dreams, the woman is still alive. The man asks a doctor to dig up his wife's body. He wants her taken out of her coffin to see if she is still alive. The doctor refuses to do it.

The man continues having dreams that his wife is alive. He asks the doctor again to check on her. The doctor refuses. The man still has the dreams. He keeps talking to the doctor. The doctor finally agrees to dig up the woman's body.

When the coffin is unlocked, they find the woman dead with her eyes wide open. Her fingernails are twisted and there are scratches on the lid of the coffin. It was as if she tried to escape from the coffin, but could not do it.

Some people may tell this legend with the husband being buried alive.

Because of modern technology, it is extremely rare to be buried alive today.

149

Number of people who were buried alive in the 1600s.

- A husband dreams that his dead wife is alive.
- He asks a doctor to take her out of her grave to check.
- When they open the coffin, they find her with her eyes open.
- She also tried to scratch her way out of the coffin.

THE TRUTH ABOUT BEING BURIED ALIVE

In Chirnside, Scotland, in 1674, Marjorie Halcrow Erskine was buried in a shallow grave. Someone opened her coffin to steal her jewelry. The woman woke up. It is very difficult for people to be buried alive today. Before people are buried, their bodies are embalmed. Anyone who is alive before burial would not survive this process. Also, there is medical equipment that checks people's vital signs. This allows doctors to find out if someone is still alive. After this process, a doctor has to pronounce someone dead.

A Woman Tans Too Much

A young woman is going on vacation. She wants to get a great tan beforehand. She goes to a local tanning salon. She finds out she can lay on the tanning bed only for a certain amount of time each day. This is not enough time to get her skin the color she wants. She decides to go to every tanning salon in town.

Later, the woman notices her skin smells funny. She bathes often and uses perfume. But the smell will not go away. The woman goes to the doctor to find out what is happening. He tells her the tanning rays cooked her internal organs. She has only a few weeks left to live.

In another version of this tale, a woman is about to get married. She wants to get a tan so she looks better in her wedding dress. She visits every tanning salon in town. They tell her she can tan for only

Spending too much time in tanning beds can cause skin cancer.

THINK ABOUT IT

Do you think it is important to look good? Would you put your health at risk for looks? What do you think about the woman in this urban legend?

30

Time, in minutes, that the tanning salons tell a woman she could tan.

- A woman wants a deep tan for her vacation.
- She visits all of the town's tanning salons in one day.
- She notices a funny smell that will not go away.
- The tanning cooked the woman's internal organs.

30 minutes, two times a week. The woman wants to tan more than that. She goes to all the local tanning salons and spends 30 minutes at each one.

The woman gets married. She is a beautiful bride with a deep tan. After the ceremony, her husband says she has an unusual smell. When they go on their honeymoon, the smell does not go away. It gets worse throughout the vacation. The woman goes to the hospital. Doctors cannot figure out why she smells so bad. Then the woman gets very sick and dies. When the doctors examine her body, they find out her internal organs had been cooked. This story began to spread in 1987.

The legend says the bride cooked her organs by tanning.

A Can of Snakes Hurts Fishing Boy

Two men walk near a stream. They see a young boy fishing. He has a can of worms next to him. The men ask the child how the fish are biting. He says, "The fish aren't biting so well, but the worms sure are." The two men laugh and walk away. They thought the boy's answer was strange.

Later that day, the men walk back along that same stream. They find the boy dead. It is discovered that the can next to the boy was filled with baby rattlesnakes, not worms. The snakes bit him. He was poisoned and died.

There are other versions of this story. In one tale, a sheriff sees a boy fishing. He also asks how the fish are biting. The boy says the same thing to him. Later, the sheriff wonders what the boy

The two men do not see the venomous snakes in the boy's bucket.

was talking about. He drives back to check on him. He sees that the boy has snakebites all over his body. The can was filled with copperhead snakes. People started telling this urban legend in the 1950s.

In another outdoor urban legend, a man is hiking. A rattlesnake bites him through one of his hiking boots. The man dies. His wife keeps his belongings for a long time. One day, she decides to sell his things in a yard sale. A young man at the sale looks at the hiking boots. He tries them on. He feels a bad pain in his foot and dies a few minutes later. The rattlesnake's fangs are still in the boots, and they poisoned him.

2
Number of men who walked past a young boy fishing.

- A boy fishing has a can of worms next to him.
- A few men ask him how the fish are biting.
- They later find the boy dead.
- There were baby rattlesnakes in the can, not worms.

Copperhead snakes are one of the most venomous snakes.

A Dress Poisons a Young Girl

The story of a poisoned dress has been around for decades. In the story, a girl buys a formal dress to wear to a dance. While she is at the dance, she starts to feel sick. She goes outside to get some fresh air. It does not make her feel better. The girl later goes to the bathroom and dies.

It is later revealed that the dress came off the body of a dead girl. The dress was used for the funeral and returned to the store. The formaldehyde from the dead girl seeped into the dress. It got into the new girl's skin and killed her.

There is a more modern version of this story. A woman buys an expensive dress from a department store. She wants to be buried in

The girl has no idea the dress she bought will kill her.

it. The woman's daughter does not think it is a good idea to bury her mother in such an expensive dress. She gets the dress after her mother's funeral and returns it to the department store.

Another woman buys the same dress from the store. When she wears it, she gets a bad rash. She goes to the doctor and finds out she has been exposed to formaldehyde.

It came from the body of the first woman who had the dress.

This story became popular in the 1940s and 1950s. It was especially popular in the Midwest because there were so many expensive department stores in cities such as Chicago, Illinois; Indianapolis, Indiana; Cincinnati, Ohio; and Saint Louis, Missouri.

1930s
Era when people started telling the story of the poisoned dress.

- A girl buys a dress to wear to a dance.
- At the dance, she starts to feel sick, and later dies.
- The dress came from a dead body and had formaldehyde on it.
- A modern story says a daughter returned her dead mother's dress to a department store.

THINK ABOUT IT

Why do you think so many urban legends involve stories about young women? List three reasons.

A Spider Ruins a Woman's Vacation

A woman goes on vacation to a tropical location. While on her trip, she goes to the beach. A spider bites her cheek. The spider bite starts to bother her. Her face begins swelling up. The woman goes home so she can go to the doctor. When the doctor cuts that area of her face open, hundreds of spiders come out of the woman's cheek. The spider had laid eggs in her face.

There is another version of the story. The woman with the spider bite does not go to the doctor. When she gets home from her vacation, her face is itching. She puts cream on her cheek and forgets about the spider bite.

After a while, the woman notices her face has not healed yet. Her cheek is still itching and has turned red. It becomes uncomfortable. The woman scratches her face. Her skin cracks and hundreds of tiny spiders come out of her cheek.

This story

Spiders lay hundreds of eggs at a time.

gained popularity in the 1970s in Europe.

Another urban legend about spiders involves a cactus. In this story, a woman buys a large cactus and brings it home. There is something strange about the cactus. When the woman waters it, the cactus moves and makes strange noises. The woman calls the store where she bought the cactus to find out why it was happening. She is told to get the cactus out of her home. She later discovers the cactus is filled with spiders.

> Many people are afraid of spiders, which is why they are in many legends.

1970s
Era when the spider bite stories began to spread.

- A woman goes on vacation and a spider bites her cheek.
- Her face begins to swell and itch.
- She goes to the doctor and finds hundreds of spiders in her face.
- The spider had laid its eggs in the bite.

SPIDERS IN BUBBLE GUM

In 1977, there was a rumor about Bubble Yum brand bubble gum. Many people said this gum had spider eggs in it. The company wanted to stop the rumors. It put a full-page advertisement in newspapers, saying that there were no spider eggs in Bubble Yum. It cost a lot of money to do this. People eventually stopped spreading this rumor.

A Dream Saves a Woman from an Accident

A woman has a dream about a funeral procession passing by. It has many cars in it. She notices the man driving the hearse. Something about him stands out to her. In her dream, the man looks at her and says, "There's room for one more."

The next day, the woman goes shopping at a department store. She cannot get the dream out of her mind. The hearse driver's face is still in her head too. At the store, the woman is about to get into an elevator. It is very crowded. As she is about to get in, she notices the elevator operator. He has the same face of the man from her dream. He calls out to her, "There's room for one more." The woman runs away. The elevator falls and everyone inside is killed.

The woman runs after recognizing the elevator operator.

THINK ABOUT IT

Do you believe that your dreams can tell you what will happen in the future? Have you ever had a dream that came true?

Another version of the story involves a taxi instead of an elevator. The person who had the dream refuses to get inside a crowded taxi. Later, the taxi gets into a car accident. All the people inside are killed.

The elevator story became popular in the 1940s and 1950s. It is one of the few urban legends that involve the supernatural. People no longer tell this story today. It is not believable anymore. Department stores do not have elevator operators now.

A more updated version of the legend involves a full taxi.

1

Number of additional people that could fit in the elevator.

- A woman dreams about a funeral procession and notices the hearse driver.
- At the department store, the elevator operator looks similar to the man in her dream.
- She refuses to get on the elevator.
- It crashes and everyone is killed.

URBAN LEGEND ON TELEVISION

On February 10, 1961, *The Twilight Zone* had an episode based on this urban legend. A dancer gets sick and goes to the hospital. Every night, she dreams about a nurse. The nurse takes her to the morgue in Room 22. When the nurse opens the door, she says, "Room for one more, honey." Later, the dancer is about to get on flight number 22. She notices the flight attendant looks similar to the nurse about whom she dreamed. The flight attendant says, "Room for one more, honey." The woman runs away. The plane starts to take off and then explodes.

Fact Sheet

- The fear of spiders is called arachnophobia. People who experience arachnophobia may feel nauseous and dizzy. They may also sweat a lot and have a fast heartbeat. Arachnophobia is treated through therapy and relaxation.

- Many spiders cannot bite through human skin. Spiders have fangs that cannot pierce human flesh. What people consider spider bites actually come from other bugs, such as fleas. They may also be chemical reactions or an infection.

- Spiders will bite people only when they are defending themselves. This happens when someone scares them.

- Urban legends about Coca-Cola are called Cokelore.

- The fear of clowns is called coulrophobia. Psychologists say that one reason people are afraid of clowns is because of the makeup they wear. Also, there are many movies with scary clowns in them.

- Claustrophobia is the fear of being trapped in small places. About five percent of people in the United States suffer from this. Most of the people who have claustrophobia are women. People with claustrophobia may have chills, panic attacks, and a rapid heartbeat.

- Snakes do not smell through their noses. Their sense of smell comes from their tongues. They use their tongues to collect scent particles.

- Someone who studies snakes is called a herpetologist. They work with many reptiles and amphibians. A herpetologist may study turtles, alligators, lizards, frogs, and crocodiles.

Glossary

columnist
Someone who writes a newspaper or magazine column.

embalm
To add chemicals to a dead body so it does not decay.

folklore
Customs and stories that people pass down from generation to generation.

formaldehyde
A chemical used to preserve dead bodies.

intruder
Someone who goes somewhere without permission.

kerosene
Oil that is used for fuel.

minister
Someone who performs religious ceremonies.

morgue
A room where dead bodies are kept before burial.

procession
A line of cars that move together slowly during a ceremony.

settlement
The final payment of something.

For More Information

Books

Clay, Kathryn. *Top 10 Urban Legends*. Mankato, MN: Capstone, 2012.

Krieger, Emily. *Myths Busted! 2: Just When You Thought You Knew What You Knew*. Washington, DC: National Geographic, 2014.

Stewart, Gail B. *Urban Legends*. San Diego, CA: ReferencePoint, 2012.

Visit 12StoryLibrary.com

Scan the code or use your school's login at **12StoryLibrary.com** for recent updates about this topic and a full digital version of this book. Enjoy free access to:

- Digital ebook
- Breaking news updates
- Live content feeds
- Videos, interactive maps, and graphics
- Additional web resources

Note to educators: Visit 12StoryLibrary.com/register to sign up for free premium website access. Enjoy live content plus a full digital version of every 12-Story Library book you own for every student at your school.

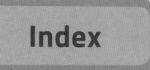

Index

About the Author

Kenya McCullum has been a fan of scary stories since she was a child. When she was a little girl, she watched many horror movies with her grandmother and loves watching them to this day. Halloween is one of her favorite holidays.

READ MORE FROM 12-STORY LIBRARY

Every 12-Story Library book is available in many formats. For more information, visit 12StoryLibrary.com.